# Gilbert and the Bicycle

*To the wildlife of Barham Moor*

Scholastic Book Services Inc.
10 Earlham Street, London WC2H 9LN, England

Scholastic Book Services
730 Broadway, New York, NY 10003, USA

Scholastic Tab Publications Ltd,
123 Newkirk Road, Richmond Hill, Ontario L4C 3G5, Canada

Ashton/Scholastic Pty Ltd, PO Box 579,
Gosford, New South Wales, Australia

Ashton/Scholastic Ltd,
165 Marua Road, Panmure, Auckland 6, New Zealand

First published in the UK by Hutchinson Junior Books Ltd, 1982
Published in paperback by Scholastic Book Services, Inc. 1984



Made and printed in Spain by Mateu Cromo, Madrid

# *Gilbert and the Bicycle*

*Jack Harvey*

**Hippo Books**
**Scholastic Book Services**
**London**

Gilbert lived on the edge of a wide pond with his family and all their friends and relations.

But Gilbert was different.

He was very small for his age and he couldn't jump very far, which made all the other frogs laugh at him.

He tried to join in all the games, but no-one would play with him.

This made Gilbert very miserable.

One day he tied a spring to his feet, but instead of leaping elegantly he made one huge hop and crashed nose-first to the ground.

All the frogs laughed so loudly their bellies ached!

Close to tears, Gilbert threw the spring away as far as he could.

'I'll leave home,' he said. 'And I won't come back until I can jump better than any of them.'

He walked and walked until he was tired. Then he flopped down under a large tree, and sniffled a bit, quietly to himself.

Suddenly, Gilbert heard a strange moaning, squeaking sound. There, walking slowly towards a clump of grass, was the strangest-looking creature he had ever seen – a roundish animal with a snout – and most curious of all, it was wheeling a bicycle!

Scared, Gilbert hid behind a stone. The noise came closer and closer until finally it stopped under the tree. Gilbert dared not move.

After what seemed hours, the moaning and sniffling died down. Gilbert could control his curiosity no longer and very quietly he peered out.

Forgetting how frightened he had been, Gilbert tip-toed up to see what was the matter. He gave a timid cough, and the creature leapt with a start.

'Who is it? What do you want?' said the animal, trembling.

'Is anything the matter?' croaked Gilbert nervously.

'Matter? Can't you see what's the matter? I've lost all my prickles!'

'Prickles! said Gilbert.

'Yes, prickles! Have you never seen a hedgehog without its prickles before?'

Gilbert was about to say he hadn't but stopped himself as the hedgehog began sobbing again.

'I'll be a laughing stock when they find I'm bald!' he snorted, shaking his head miserably.

'Don't cry,' said Gilbert in a comforting voice. 'How did you manage to lose them?'

'I was trying to ride my bicycle without any hands when I fell off and landed on my back in a muddy ditch.

I couldn't move for hours . . . and then the mud went hard in the sun. So when I finally got out, all my prickles got left behind.'

'How awful!' said Gilbert. 'Why don't the two of us go and search for a new coat of prickles?'

This cheered the hedgehog up a little. 'But where are we going to get one?' he asked.

Gilbert was stumped.

He scratched his head and paced up and down thinking hard. 'I don't know,' he said finally. 'But we'll find something.'

They came to a signpost covered with weeds and moss.

'What does it say?' asked the hedgehog.

Gilbert didn't have much of a head for heights, but he climbed up to take a closer look. 'To Meadowdale Farm,' he read.

They followed the overgrown path to the gates of the farm. Keeping their ears and eyes open for anything that moved, they peered into the yard.

It was deserted, and the only sound they could hear was the creaking of the old barn door.

'I don't like the look of this place – it gives me the creeps,' whispered the hedgehog, ready to ride off on his bicycle.

Gilbert was very afraid too, but he didn't want to give up. 'We haven't even started yet,' he pleaded.

So the hedgehog searched the barn and Gilbert climbed up some steps.

'Look! Over there!' shouted Gilbert suddenly. The hedgehog ran out of the barn as if he had seen a ghost.

‘What is it?’ he said, trying to catch his breath.

‘An old broom!’ said Gilbert, grinning. ‘It’s just what we need!’

‘You are clever,’ said the hedgehog, admiringly.

Soon they were pulling out the bristles until they had an armful each.

‘That should be enough,’ said the hedgehog. ‘Now let’s get out of here before somebody catches us!’

They tied the bristles to the bicycle and pushed it back up the hill.

At the top they sat down.

‘All that work for nothing!’ groaned the hedgehog.

Gilbert looked puzzled.

‘How are you going to glue the bristles on?’ said the hedgehog gloomily.

Gilbert hadn’t given that a thought. They both sat there in silence.

'I'm a failure, after all,' muttered Gilbert to himself. But then an idea struck him.

At the nearest ditch, he began covering the hedgehog with lumps of mud.

'It's worth a try!' he said determinedly.

Then, picking up the bristles one by one, he stuck them neatly over his friend's back.

'Wait for the mud to dry and you'll be as good as new,' said Gilbert. 'This new coat will last until your prickles grow again.'

The hedgehog looked at his reflection in the stream nearby. 'Oh! How can I ever thank you?' he cried.

'I know, you can have my bicycle! Don't say no – I insist. It's yours for keeps.'

Gilbert was overjoyed.

'Well, I must be going now,' said the hedgehog, 'or my family will be worrying about me. Goodbye; perhaps we'll meet again,' and off he skipped over the meadow, whistling happily to himself.

It was beginning to get dark. Gilbert felt lonely again and very small. What should he do? He still couldn't hop any further than when he had set out that afternoon.

Then he remembered his bicycle and he felt better.

'After all,' he said to himself, 'I can ride on two wheels as fast as any frog can leap on two legs.' And with this comforting thought he set off, rather shakily, for home.

He reached the top of the hill overlooking the pond, when suddenly he heard a great crying and shouting below . . .

A heron was hunting and all the frogs were running for their lives. But one frog had hurt his leg and he couldn't hop fast enough to get away.

'Help! Save me!' croaked the frog as the heron towered over him.

Without stopping to think, Gilbert headed his bicycle straight for the heron.

He pedalled frantically down the hill.

Just as the heron was about to strike, Gilbert snatched the frog from under its very beak, and raced away.

His only chance now was to head for the thicket where the heron couldn't follow.

'Faster! He's gaining on us!' cried the frog as the bird's shadow loomed over them.

With one last effort, Gilbert vanished into the tangle of grass bushes. The heron gave a squawk of anger. He had lost them, and he flew off, furious.

Immediately the other frogs hopped over to see if they were safe.

Gilbert was scared they might laugh when they saw him with his bicycle, but they didn't. Instead, they carried him on their shoulders croaking, 'Three cheers for Gilbert – hip-hip-hooray!'

And several of them asked rather shyly if he would teach them how to ride.